Existence

Playing with Creation

Aquiles Chan

* * *

Second edition: 2017

E-mail: camilosiu@hotmail.com

ISBN-13:
978-1545499269

ISBN-10:
1545499268

DEDICATION

I give thanks to the luck that I have had during my life. I am very grateful with my mother, for her decisions of convincing our father to send us to the greatest universities of the world had positive results at the end. I was lucky to be sent to the University of California in Berkeley.

I am very grateful because this experience made me change my way of living and thinking. The quality of its professors and classmates made me be infected of their knowledge. This is why I'm thankful for my mother and the University of California in Berkeley for making me feel like one of the luckiest and happiest man of my time.

TABLE OF CONTENTS

Chapter 1

Chapter 11

Chapter 111

CHAPTER 1

THEORY ABOUT THE EXISTENCE
WITH IMAGE OF THE CREATOR

2011's original radio microwave photograph from the WMAP according to NASA. Everything that is existence included inside this sphere. The entire cosmos is limited inside this sphere.

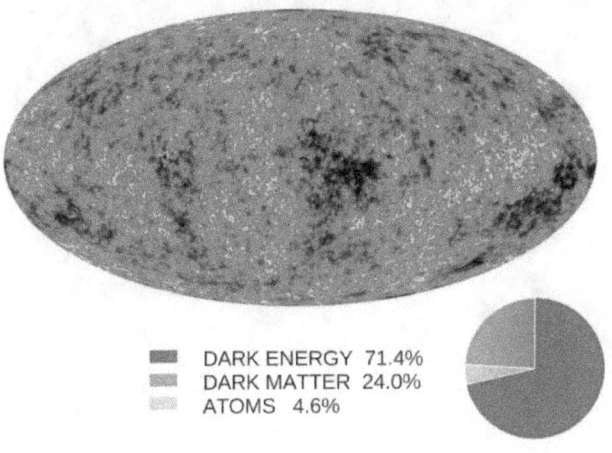

DARK ENERGY 71.4%
DARK MATTER 24.0%
ATOMS 4.6%

A radio section of the sphere

A theory about Existence

Where do we come from? What is the purpose of our individual existence and where will we be in the infinite future? How can we find "the answers"? There have been many, but the truth is up until now, they all have been governed by three main ideologies: the scientific ideology, the religious ideology and the philosophical ideology.

These ideologies, with their political and social powers, with arguments or without them, have prevented the emergence of new theories and perspectives which may introduce better prospects with good standards of credibility. *Scientific* theory attracts the greatest number of enthusiasts.

Celebrating Nobel Prizes on red carpets, who receive outrageous fortunes that facilitate machinery which enables them to observe and assess the objects and particles of the universe. Without a shadow of a doubt, those machines were partly responsible for $E=MC2$, the atomic energy, which made World War II come to an end and gave rise to a new era. To scientists, metaphysics has none relevance whatsoever, "the conscious soul, with free will, does not exist". Every action comes from a previous one. Every reaction stems from a random coincidence, mathematically calculable.

Notwithstanding all the resources available to them, they have yet to decipher "the living and conscious soul of their being" as that of the greatest value and importance within their spiritual human ego.

The egocentric thinking of greater concern among most individuals is to believe, as scientists do, that when we pass away we transform into energy, and if we were to come back to the world of the living, we would be elements in some other organism, with no memory of our own. That all around us turns into a physicochemical reality, when our "self" submerges back into the complete and obscure inexistence.

The theory of the author, and the chief objective of this book, counteracts those "self-centered negative feelings" with a positive reasoning, without being endorsed by divine or scientific arguments. The basis sustained is that "death" does not exist. Being the time cyclical and infinite, there is no reason to support that something can be created from inexistence nor that something existent may go back into nothing. Should there be any need for a Creator or a God to exist, it would be unreasonable that Him, perfect and just as he were to be, could have created "poor or slave people", to whom he will cause death, even after having them suffered on Earth, and to whose soul he will punish in the most terrible way we could possibly imagine: an everlasting inferno.

The creation of the eternal would eradicate the concept of the *cyclical existence*, in which what is not cyclical cannot be eternal.

The book as a whole will explain how the author has been able to encounter peace in his inner self, and how to appreciate what exists around us as a continuous paradise; to believe in existence as something where my inner "self" is eternal, leaving no possibility to vanish for being part of the eternal original matter.

For its part, while science is the main contributor to discoveries and manufactures, *religion* is the main consumer and user. Its ideologies are the chief influence in politics. They are the cause of most wars and human disasters. Almost every religion base their theory of the origin on a god completely different from the human being. You shall never reveal an opinion about him, under penalty of earthly death and a second spiritual death doomed to everlasting infernos. Only his preachers have the right to construe and transmit the desires of their Creator.

Many religions have discovered the magic formula of the absolute power over its supporters. What "E=MC2" means to scientists is what "disobedience = eternal inferno" means to many religions. "Disobedience" only in the eyes of the "owners" of certain creeds.

Philosophers or semi-philosophers, such as Hindus, Buddhists, Pantheist and some others who do not believe in an alien Creator different from our being, feel existence, in its entirety, as something "living": the only thing that truly matters, above everything else we can imagine. Not only do we share such value, but we feel it as something that belongs to us until it becomes an integral part of our "self". Therefore, every event in the making of existence is also our personal event, just as much in experience as in importance.

Several of these philosophers believe that the present life is part of an event where, if we meditate to clear our minds of the mundane such as the negative mental state, we may reach a liberating peace, and through such serenity, on the onset of death, we may not have to reincarnate in this valley of pain and tears. By doing so, we accomplish our integration to the ONE and the liberation of Karma: peace and quiet for all the eternity. The author does not agree with these last ideas.

Baruch Spinoza was the first philosopher to originate the Pantheistic Monism ideas of the Modern times.

He considered that all is God. Including us, tangible things, nature and all its matters. He also justified good and evil with his ethical thinking, which is a coordination between spiritual state with the Creator and matter. He does not believe in evil itself. He does not believe in punishments of infernos nor in eternal paradises rewards.

He believes that evil is to be compensated with good. These religions or philosophies have two significant comparative basis:

1. They all consider the "original" of "All" as a *unique being*, isolated, the origin within which we find existence. They agree that this being is omnipotent and that he can do whatever his imagination desires. Is that whose nature encloses existence.

   What exists on its own and it shall be conceived disconnected to anything else. That it has prevailed through the infinite past and that it shall continue to exist for all the eternal future.

2. The most important distinction between Monist and Pantheistic ideology as opposed to Dualist and Theist ideology is that, when human beings were created, Pantheistic Monism considered that in such creation the Creator and all that was created are one and the same matter with an integrated spirit. Dualists religions only accept that the Creator, for being perfect, has a different matter than human beings, for them being imperfect.

For the time being, none of these ideologies have bothered to use a different reasoning in analyzing the relation between the "Perfect Immortal" with his creation of the imperfect mortal. Most of them begin with a story that will later become history. Almost all of them have used intimidation as a means to conviction (the two deaths). In this work, the author presents an unprecedented imaginary hypothesis about the "purpose" of the Creator towards that created.

He considers that if we can demonstrate a consistent "purpose" for "before" and "after", we may logically explain the present. The author states that if there have been infinite universal events through time and so there will be some other infinite events in the future, then our present cannot be the first, the only or the last one.

Thus, neither the events in the past, the future nor our present can cease completely and permanently (with eternal paradises or infernos). They shall always conclude with events that lead to openings for the following possible event. Furthermore, those of us who participate in an event are part of Him, acting as the neurons of his macro brain. We will be an important piece, taking part in his feeling as a sole being, in experience and thought. We shall not be like an insignificant object, comparable to a nail or a piece of cloth.

For what reason do each of us detach from the All in the ideology of Spinoza. Being disengaged from the One will make us feel individual beings, with free will. In this fashion, we endow with greater excitement the macro existence.

Among some other liberties that our Creator conferred in humans, we find the freedom of action, according to which the future of every move cannot be defined. In other words, the One is unable to know the action he will do in the future, neither his own nor of any other participant.

He installed in humans the ignorance of death, the doubts about their future existence. However, he did leave the knowledge of numerical results, the concept of infinite related to the concept of "the all". In this way, I consider that "The All" created a universe to "play with its creation". It introduced positivism, providing, to all participants, reasons to feel pleasant emotions (us included), in such a way that they could experience justice, equity, to counteract the universal events that may otherwise lapse into a tedious inertia, repeating our grand existence.

The One may have created heaven similar to the paradise created for Adan and Eve, or similar to those eternal paradises promised by many religious people.

However, thinking logically about the paradise of the Eden couple, anyone could deduce that, without the introduction of "the apple", this paradise would not exist for not agreeing with the concept of "eternity".

Without emotions (the apple), it would be a lifeless paradise, idle, no art, no objects, no reason to exist. Having said this, my hope is that my readers find an alternative to ponder on this philosophy and to further feel the absolute pantheism in which we all participate of the eternal matter. Consequently, we all are eternal. Death is a transitory experience, not eternal.

Neither nothing, from nothing, can become "something"; nor can "something" existing vanish into nothing.

My theory about existence also agrees with millennial ideas of these philosophies which state that an inner instinct of human beings knows that everything has always existed and that we are a part of the Creator. Therefore, if we now feel that we are individually isolated, logic leads us to believe that we will all return to the unit so that we can feel that we are a single Being, the One, cyclically.

Having this intuitive support which stems from long generations of millennial societies, I cherish the main foundations of this theory as a set of ideas justified by the millions of people who have lived before us, thus classifying them as believable and possible, true within human imagination.

Which ideology is the most important to our "self"? The "self" is the most important in any event. Almost every time what matters most to us is what our "self" is experiencing or about to experience. Almost no one cares what is happening to other people in the world just as long as, in that moment, is not affecting them. This may seem a poor moral teaching, but what I intend to transmit is that *the value human beings place in facts depends on what each of them consider relevant.*

An example could be the night that Neil Armstrong landed on the moon. My TV had collapsed. So I went to my neighbor´s house. She was watching a soap-opera of forbidden love affairs. My wife and I implored her to change the channel. She refused. But with the help of her husband and her three children she bitterly agreed. When Neil first step on the moon, the six of us started to scream with joy euphorically, like everybody else.

My bitter neighbor, reluctantly persuaded by her children, sat on her kitchen and ate a cucumber.

When we were all shouting exhilarated, we could hear from the kitchen: "All I care is my cucumber, I could not care less that gringo is playing with the moon". Building on this, I can state that I do mind more about the ideas of the science and religions than the value of a cucumber; I will focus my utmost attention to the "self", to our "soul", supporting it as the most important element within the whole existence.

~~~

Aquiles Chan Theory

I shall introduce the complete theory concisely to emphasize the main objective analyzed above. The solitary origin of the all is the so called Creator, which comprises the whole existence. In the existence we find the abstract matter and senses, such as the human conscience. The Creator, logically, has always existed, timeless, eternal.

This fact is the most important basis of this theory, since if we are formed and transformed with parts of such Creator, we are the components of an eternal essence, hence we have always existed and we are eternal as well.

Through the passage of time, this solitary Creator is not exempt from having to present *movement* activities, those which give a sense of *life*. *Ennui* forces him to give a meaning to existence. He needs to start creating activities with a sense of life. *Life* requires participants to have *free will*. Such freedom is unbreakable law, mandatory even to the Creator.

The obligations of the "participants" in this existence consist in each of them acting with total freedom so as to create an artistic and exciting "biography", different from all the rest. I consider that all of us, the participants, have come to have fun "playing with our creation". Scientists have accurately estimated that all of our acts, movements, voices and possibly our thoughts are being recorded in our environment.

The reason of this phenomenon, according to the author, is that in the end of our current universal event, each participant will use their part recorded in the environment to tell everyone present his or her original biography. The fact that everything is present in all the environment will make the audience, once immersed in the biography, personify and live the narration. In this way, each of us, as a member of the All-encompassing, will experience the feelings of pleasure or suffering already recorded with the current speaker.

I grant this argument about the purpose of our existence two significant positive connotations. Firstly, being time infinite, it is necessary that the

Creator presents creations that inspire great emotions to His and all of the participants' pleasure. It would also be unreasonable that if the Creator fabricates creations to "spend time", he would do them with negativism. It is completely natural for him to do it positively, always. He would never dare create eternal infernos.

Being as perfect as He is, he could only do positive things, and could never, even if he would want to, do negative things.

It all must be about the real reasons that give sense to *life*, with enough creativity so that at no point in the infinite timeline may the boredom factor prevail, the meaning of which is inertia with a tilt toward inexistence or *death of existence.*

Secondly, being each and every one of us a part of the *Origin of the All*, none of us will feel as an injustice the fact of having participated in the *earthly theatre* in a slightly more unpleasant, painful and less glorious presentation, compared to some else's biography, who were, since birth, great celebrities, wealthy, powerful and who have never suffered terrible diseases till their last day.

In that *"Final Judgement"* all of them will live, vividly, the life of them all. Those will indeed be great moments of intense emotions.

The most relevant point is that, in the end, when each of us return to the *Origin of All*, none of us may claim to the One the biography he or she was given the opportunity to present. Precisely, all of them will experience living your life as you will experience living theirs. Further on, when returning to the *sphere of the all*, no participant will feel "death" or their inexistence. We will all feel our merging to the all so that we can feel a single being. In Pantheistic terms, we, all together, will become again a single Creator. Immediately prepared to the next "Big Bang", or new creation of the universe as it will be repeatedly through the eternal infinite.

The beginning of the "All". Let us analyze what must have existed first: Was it the matter or tangible energy defined by scientists, the particles of which are the early stages of the atom? Or was it the "dark energy", already outlined and acknowledged in our Cosmos by those same scientists?

They have been unable to find a formula that allows them to analyze this yet abstract "energy". I consider that what first existed was the "dark energy". As a whole, I deem it to be a "living" energy, with a thinking mind and conscience of a being with a "soul" (secular), an independent being, with free will and the awareness of being the unique beginning of it all, with the power to transform at its sole discretion everything ever imagined. A thinking being who may create "something" out of his sole imagination. Yet a tangible inert matter could have never created a thinking living matter. Philosophically, I conclude that, logically speaking, "the dark thinking living energy" existed first than the "scientific tangible inert energy".

This *"dark energy"* is like water to fish, like air to birds and the environment where all that is tangible and abstract navigates through the whole Cosmos. Scientists agree that this energy, added to the dark matter, occupy more that 95% of the entire cosmic space. I regard the total amount of this energy as a single being, a unit, as the only unit aware of its individuality.

I will refer to it as the "One", the "Creator", "the Original All", existing since the infinite past, currently in the present, and in the eternal future. I named it the All for being comparable to a large brain where everything imaginable, including us, current mortal humans, participate the same way the neurons do in the brain. In this united entity of the all, when we disengage from it to be momentarily sole individuals, for being living our present, we acquire the feeling of being independent, free and separate of the "Original All".

With our free will and responsibility for our future actions, we enter the "earthly life" so that each of us, in this theatrical event, can freely prepare a biography to be reported to the One, once our cyclical universal event or our Big Bang is completed. Later on I shall further explain how this "purpose of our current universal event" has, philosophically, reason to be "true and accurate".

The reasons relate to the attempt to conclude the cycle with a perfect justice of feelings, equal to all participants, and with the fulfillment of all our personal expectations, honoring payment for remorse for all mistakes made, and gaining, as reward, heavenly glory and pleasures.

The hypotheses where one is born a "sinner" have no logical support. It is equally illogical and unfair to believe that if indigenous communities secluded in the Amazon do not "insert" or "baptize" they should be subject to segregation and punishment for all eternity.

In this sense, the author, in "Playing with creation", hopes to present to you a reasonable option about his theory about existence, based upon the fact that we are all immortal because we come from the "immortal energy", that every emotion is positive and where we all participate relishing our true, believable and logically just purposes.

An alternative scientific argument supporting our immortality is that our universal event is cyclical. This present event is not the only nor the final one. Egocentrism has always been a human flaw. First they asserted, under penalty of political death to the opponents, that the sun and all celestial bodies of the universe revolve around our planet. Later on, that the earth was flat. And last but not least, that we are the only living beings in the Cosmos.

Scientists have already acknowledged that every Big Bang was preceded by infinite others, and that they will be equally followed by infinite more, throughout the entire eternity.

For a better understanding, in my imagination I cut a fragment of this straight timeline and connect one opposite end to the other, thus obtaining the shape of a large finite circle. Therewith, I shape a cyclical circle in which I can distinguish the totality without having a "beginning or ending" point of time-space.

I designed this diagram to refer to the following ones, not as a linear infinite, but as a finite circle in which one may always move forward, infinitely, in the time cycle. It is not reasonable to believe that, in the end of our universal chapter, we arrive at a situation in which the beginning of the subsequent creation is not allowed. It necessarily has to be a continuous, neutral, just, perfect and logical ending.

The Cosmos, The Big Bang, Disintegration, by science, by the author

Our galaxy comprehends the space of the solar system. The Cosmos contains the complete set of galaxies. The Universe comprehends the Cosmos plus all of what scientists classify as "calculable presences". Finally, "the Existence" encompasses the entire infinite space and everything imaginable, whether inside or out of our multiple dimensions. According to scientists, the Big Bang started to disintegrate from a nanoparticle, when all particles began to separate from each other. It is not merely about an explosion in which a core spark caused the all to zoom off from that initial point of explosion.

Lately, scientists observe that a "dark energy" is continuously filling empty spaces. All the things disassociate from all the rest. The effects increase each time. According to estimations, this expansion seems like an endless cycle. Inasmuch as they expand, they lose energy as well, therefore, they will lose mass. According to scientific calculations, our "sun" loses mass by the minute, and everything inside our galaxy loses mass as well to become pure energy (MC2=E). Therefore, our galaxies will not attract each other again to become the initial nanoparticle. It will all develop into dissipated energy within the limits of our Cosmos.

The diameter of this Cosmos has already been calculated. What is important is that they accept it has limits, whole-map of the Cosmos or WMAP. Astrophysicists agree that the Cosmos dimensions are finite, measurable and verifiable.

Considerable concentrations of movable energy have been found inside this "dark energy". Some argue that once everything that was originated by the Big Bang becomes pure energy, then, the "living" clouds of energy will begin to swirl inside this new Cosmos (the author interprets this as brain activity in a working state of mind) to generate a gigantic "black hole", in which everything around it will compress and produce, once more, a super condensed nanoparticle, just as ours was. Thus, the following Big Bang will start once again (approved by scientists), until the end of these days, as it was in the eternity of past days.

The author abides to scientific facts as unvarnished truth. Using them as pillar, he portrays them in a different manner. I ratify as real the figures of its diameter. I ratify the fact that it has boundaries that prevent the traffic in and out of it. I ratify the fact that minutes before the explosion of the Big Bang, the whole sphere was pure energy with a homogeneous consistency. And I ratify the fact that the energy clouds were moving to form a big black hole.

I explain the above mentioned in this other way: our grand sphere of the One is the cosmic sphere. The swirling movements are nothing but the moments in which our One is activating the brain to think. The nanoparticle is the beginning in which the energy is transformed into tangible matter. The most relevant aspect in this event is that scientists uphold that this creation has been generated by accidental clashes of the Cosmos.

The author contends that this is evidence of brain functions of the One, and that the outcome are decisions made with the free will of *a being* fully aware of his existence, as we, human beings, sense it inside our brains.

Immediately after the explosion of the Big Bang, "Who" created the "laws of physics?" Behold the major question that has started almost every religious origins, with their consequent wars and struggles for social power.

I propose the One as the Creator of all forthcoming events. Scientists and religious people alike agree that this single argument is properly logic. The beginning must arise from a single starting point or a solitary *being*, without "something" surrounding it. It has been unanimously agreed that there was a "Who" that created everything around us, it only remains to decipher who is that "Who". The answer will always rest at the discretion of each society. The following question would be: "Why, what was the purpose of this master piece?"

I resolve that the *"macro existence"* needs to exist actively moving. Should existence cease its activity for one moment, it would present, as scientists say: a complete depletion of the "moving power", thus, if there is no other engine to start the first original impulse in the whole cosmic space, the absolute existence would remain stagnant, lifeless, or in utter death, with no possibility to exist again, in all eternity. Consequently, this "Entity" has the obligation and the need to create new "laws of physics" continuously, to provide all the universes to be created, and thus keeping "apathy" at bay, creating them very similar to the previous universes.

I request mutual respect to all the philosophies presented, with all due respect to the different religions or ideologies. I do not depreciate nor comment them. I respect their fantasies and I hope to be equally respected. I request that we all respect the reader, the only one who is entitled to decide which ideas are more believable and which more disposable.

Starting by the ONE

Before the Big Bang, the Creator had to be the only existence inside the whole spherical "dark energy". Nothing had yet been isolated within Her to be molded in some form of tangible matter. Once the pieces were divided to become the particles of the atom, the One gave the orders or "physics laws" according to which they should behave. A curious fact to think about is how each atom of the Cosmos moves its electrons, all at a same speed, and have its physics laws all react in a perfectly obedient manner, without the need to be assisted by a *Master of Ceremony* to achieve such perfect control.

The following formations and evolutions of the inanimate matter are what scientists deduced with verifiable mathematical formulas. The most important stage, where the inert material with "a mysterious action" comes "to live" thus far, has been utterly refused. In line with this theory, the author uses philosophical imagination in a likely scenario to give the following opinion: the One, along with everything that is being created, are immersed in a finite *sphere* of "dark energy" (our Cosmos, WMAP). Therefore, it is simple to conceive the formation of the components of a chromosome when they are all perfectly aligned.

Afterwards, the will of the Creator shall be made allowing that with a "spark", some of the "dark energy" permeate and take control indicating such chromosome how to shape the body, the limbs, and the head with its brain, depending on the living species.

The influence that our One exercises in indicating a certain molecule of water to behave in the same way as another molecule that is more than ten billion light years away, as much in its dance of orbital electrons as in its physical reactions, proves to us that this phenomenon is only possible if everything is intended by a single director.

Our universe functions in perfect order. Not a single atom from a galaxy, with reference to another, rebels to originate a universal chaos. Should this happen, nothing could be verifiable nor recognized as "real" by our scientists.

Not only we are amazed by these relationships and coordination between each universal particle, but also they are our mental ground to distinguish between what is real and what is not. The human intuition in which everything stems from a single "Originator" is so important to us that, in order to uphold our personal opinion, we go to great lengths to dominate the submissive, and to destroy those who our military strength allows. This last statement is a serious mistake of the human beings. It is a chaos that must be rectified.

To conclude, the author suggests a culture similar to those practiced in India, the foundations of which are the respect for personal beliefs and the tendency to bolster their convictions through practices focused on the benefit of the personal "self", without intervening in what does not concern us.

In this fashion, what first existed was a single "dark living energy". She made the decision to initiate a creation so as not to "get bored". She took one part of herself (such as a brain neuron) and isolated it completely from her reach in order to create an independent being, with sheer free will.

This human shall elaborate a biography completely unexpected by the Creator. In this way, He may enjoy an unscheduled adventure, as he would do with electronic robots. In the end of the event, he will gather all his "neurons" (humans) to relish on each of their biographies. Each human, when returning to the original brain, shall not feel inexistence (death), since he is an integral part of the One.

All of us, united, will feel like a single entity with its entire existence. In other words, in the One, all of us, humans, shall feel once more like a single Being (the Creator). In order to create human beings, it is introduced, in their "fertilization", the "spark" that absorbs from the environment the "original and eternal matter", our sense of individual life which includes the power of free will, fully responsible for our actions. In this event, the Creator also decided not to be able to perceive what a singular human being will perform in his future action. On the contrary, should the Creator anticipate every action of the human beings, the entire creation of the current universal event would make no sense at all, no active aim, no reasonable purpose of true positive emotions. I do not agree with the mathematical formulas of Einstein or Hawking, in which we are all like billiard balls and all our moves have been predetermined by a prior movement or action, this would eradicate completely the free will of humans.

Once our earthly material paradise was created, they began to metaphorically write the first events of our ancestors (one of these writings is in the Bible). The Creator, by means of mutations, refined a human being who he called Adan. With him and his aid they rehearse every emotion that future generations would have to experience in order to create variations of a specific biography for all of those yet to be born. He placed Adan in a paradise where no animal, insect, plant or any remaining living beings could ever hurt or inflict suffering to him.

Adan lived thousands of years in this way, until he was introduced to the "tedium" disease. He urged the Creator a companion to remedy the feeling of "anguish and solitude". The feelings of the forthcoming humans were perfected with the creation of the woman as the most attractive and beautiful being in the planet, Eve. The delivery of Eve was the most significant motivation and exciting sensation to the upcoming humankind. With her, the most positive feelings rose, art, antidepressant, anti-solitude, and above all, the feeling of belonging that each attribute to one another: love, the highest value in human appreciation.

Our couple prospered in this paradise for many thousands of years. Nowadays, many religious people kill and die for that vague promise of being rewarded with something similar to that place where Adan and Eve lived all those blossom events.

The evidence, that proves that our couple and the Creator were only rehearsing, lies in the fact that this idyll came to an end with the inevitable: "tedium". Relentless repetition, toward an eternity, in any event of existence implies "inertia". Simultaneously, this implies inactivity toward infinite, "tedium, death of the living, flaw in existence". Our founding fathers had better prospects than the requirements claimed by our present religious communities.

The latest demand a paradise for all eternity, incurring in the error of misunderstanding the biblical parable about the "original sin". Obtaining a golden paradise replete of slaves, men or women, of the opposite or equal sex, shall always entail the entry of the inevitable army of "tedium".

Should the dreams of these "saved persons" become true, they would be locked in their golden palaces brimming with orgies, only to live in the most cruel of all infernos; the inferno of monotony and eternal tedium.

The wisdom of the architects of mankind is indisputable for their contribution to art and volatility.

After years of experience and meditation, Adan and Eve summoned the Creator to inform about the culmination of all the sentiments they would instill in human beings, the positive and the negative ones, a future with infinite events, incredible behaviors, of sentimental humilities and resignations as well as of merciless murders, loaded with greed, with their wealthy fortunes drawn from the "poor" by means of corruption as politicians, millionaires, lawyers and more.

Eve was the first one to make a comment to the Creator.

She advised the formula to introduce all these elements in the forthcoming humans: the awareness of the "earthly death". Adan added that they were not to be allowed to know in their minds about their true existence after death, they should hesitate whether "yes" or "no". He argued that these feelings would make them kind, greedy, selfish and ruthless with their fellows. Doubt entitles "preachers" to uphold that they have been chosen by their God to preach the "truthful or correct interpretation of his sacred texts".

After persuading them, they turn them into armies to kill and take ownership of the property and lives of the believers, vulnerable and devoid of individual character. Eve added envy and vanity.

These feminine features incite us to gear up more fashionable and thus, provoking others to surmount them. This is how they have passed on to us this world of fashion, excess, envy and more, and they have evolve into original motives to enjoy it in this life, as real and buoyant purposes in our creation. By doing so, our "parents" started to add both positive and negative feelings toward the behavior we would have.

The first legislative meeting was thereby closed, and the Creator approved all in the agenda, assigning the couple executive duties to begin with the reforms.

The meeting was adjourned and the Creator confirmed them that, since they were given the power of "free will", that is to say, complete responsibility for their actions and consequential results, He rendered them "the apple" with all its powers so that, when they decided to, they would initiate "humankind with all their positive and negative emotions". He also congratulate them on the ideas about the secrets concealed from humans, which aims "suggested by them" complied with all the purposes of creation.

The eternal purpose of existence cannot have a "finite end" (an end with a heavenly paradise or an eternal inferno). It must allow, in the last moment of the final event, a "happy and positive" ending, which will, thus, consequently give consent to move to the next chapter without having something "unresolved" in the previous one, something illogical and unjust (the original sin).

This reasoning is based upon a profound meditation on the true meaning of the word "eternity", constant and permanent.

As mentioned above, *the solutions for each of these events shall be found* in each participant (he, you, I, and all the rest) will elaborate a biography of our lives and the lives of everyone else. Upon the moment of the earthly death, each of us shall present before the "original sphere" in a final congregation (metaphorically defined as Final Judgement) where each will tell their story, so that all the "audience" can "live" every positive or negative emotion of the presenter and, thus, each of us could be able to "revive" every feeling of the presenter speaking at that moment.

Since we emerge from that "dark energy" as parts of it, we shall return to the One in order to restore such "borrowed" piece, similar to the return of a neuron to its original brain. In said return, we shall not feel the disappearance or death as an individual event, but instead, since we integrate as a single entity, that is, as a part of the One, we would feel entirely as a single Being unique and eternal in the Cosmos. We would not feel the inexistence, we will sense a complete union to the Brain for being integrated and belonging to the same One.

The perfect justice. It makes a good purpose for all of us to be leading authors, directors and actors in our own individual movie; this would fulfill the highest emotion to such great effort in our creation. In those moments, when we all start to "see vividly" the life of each other, lived by all of us, we shall personify Cleopatra, and her slaves, Hitler, and those exterminated by him, the artists in their most glorious moments, the wretched men and women whose only option was suicide. We shall experience every life, including the lives of the aborted and neglected to public dumpsters. Emotions will be sensed in the gaps between one biography and the following one.

We will have the exact feeling we have when we finish a movie in which we were all moved by our passions, both positive and negative, however we wake up relieved in the end, brimming with emotion, within the truth of our real eternal existence. Once "The Judgement" is completed, none of us may claim the One for participating and having suffered or relished less than someone else. Having achieved everyone´s satisfaction equally just, each of us may return to be reunited with the One to rest and prepare to the following Big Bang, and thus start, once more, "playing with creation".

The couple left "the apple" dangling, to contemplate what to do with it. They secluded themselves for several millennia until "the sin" of existence dominated them one more time: "tedium".

In a moonless night, bombarded by thunders, in the dark, an uneasy Eve informed Adan about her decision to begin the "bite of the apple". And so they did. There followed darkest nights and days with thunders and flashes of lightings; our fathers felt, for the very first time, cold and fear. They sheltered in a cave. After several months, the day awoke with a glowing sun. They surfaced with a child in their arms, and thus the procreation of our species began.

Mankind continue evolving up to where it stands today. Acting in society, it never used logic as when it acts as an individual entity. They are now marching toward their own extinction. He thinks he is smart enough to prepare a journey to another planet and then evacuate the surplus population. A population which is growing, today, exponentially and in apocalyptic directions. The advocates of such suicidal movement are the 0.01% who controls more than 60% of the global economy.

These are the billionaires who, out of pure envy, go to outrageous lengths to appear in social media as one of the top 5 most powerful people and, if possible, become "the wealthiest among the wealthier".

Next in these race of destruction we find the "powerful" politicians, the bankers, the commercial and industrial monopolists and religious people, whose fortunes place them among that 0.01% of savages. In the year 1900, humankind had a population of 1650 million people. In 1950, the population reached 2629 million (59%).

A growth of 19 million people per year. In 2000 the population rose to 6070 million. An increase of 68 million per year. According to statistics, in the year 2050 we will be 9651 million. An annual growth of 71 million.

Since the origin of human race, estimated in 7 million years, until the year 1900, population only reached 1650 million. In merely 116 years, we have reached figures surpassing the 8 billion. If no apocalyptic event occurs, to the year 2100, 15.345 million people will survive (more than twice the number we exist now).

What can we do? Start packing our bags and move to Mars? Continue listening to religious communities who claim that every child brings joy and hope to the families? I can confirm that no sacred text suggests that their God asks them to reproduce frantically.

I assume their God is limitlessly wise, thence he should have always requested them to reproduce according to the circumstances at the time. And today´s reality is *to pause* or perish. Do we really need any further evidence than the invasions of illegal immigrants are due to the overpopulation of certain countries?! They intensify the problems of the host countries, which, by fault of their politicians, withstand being illegally invaded and allow being infected by cultures in favor of "overpopulation".

The formation of slums and social ghettos has always been a steaming cauldron about to burst, for any reason without cause, in barbarian mutinies with a great number of casualties and expensive economic costs. We must contemplate what we were 50 years ago and what we will become 50 years in the future.

Without a shadow of a doubt, more than 95% of us are foreseeing that is fatally necessary to curb the exponential expansion of the world population.

The only ones who do not wish to "stop" are those contained in the 0.01%, who treat the rest of mankind as slaves, because to stop would mean the interruption of their progressive acquisitions and powers.

The interpretation of death. In the first place, to scientists, we are just as billiard balls with no "soul". Once we finish our duties, we will be discarded as robots in cosmic dumpsters. In the second place, if we listen to religious people who vindicate that we all stem from "nothing", the consequence will be that, since the future is infinite time, at some point the Creator will grow tire of our conflictive presences, thus he will return us to our allegedly origin: complete inexistence, the nothing itself. In the third place, I propose that we should drift through a calmed imagination, a profound meditation, a use of our intuition, a reminiscence, through Plato´s anamnesis, into what is logically accepted and less conflictive to our mind. What will we experience when we let live? The author believes that we will experience the crossing through a tunnel where the end is filled with light with joy.

Many of us lived with the fear of finding something negative or monstrous that makes us suffer. If we reconsider that this "ONE" is part of ourselves, then logically "HE" would not be masochistic in creating a program for its humanity with negative things.

For those instants, positivism should be programmed. The mere fact that we will feel that we are existing will be of great happiness.

The individual can remember, in his past on earth, he was tortured countless times in hearing, by true atheists, that after death there will only be "absolute non-existence".

The second great happiness will be that in that state everyone will have the knowledge of the truthful truth of all the truths ever spoken. No more the right to believe in anything that is false stories. The third happiness will be, following that one path, the encounter with his beings most remembered and loved. In those meeting will be hugs and tears of immense emotions. They will converse with almost no time limit.

On the left, one will find a place with an aspect of hell. On the right will be another place that looks like a paradise of happiness.

On this path every being that arrives, according to his beliefs, his religion, his culture, and according to his earthly behaviour, will himself walk within hell or paradise.

He would stay for a short or long time according to him, for ask for his remorse within his conscience to achieve freedom and peace for his soul. Those who look the right path will feel great satisfaction for the works they considered human and contributed to the well-being of their earthly companions.

In the end, the "ONE" within the pantheistic belief, we are all one "I" will follow the logically raised logic. We will all achieve absolute satisfaction according to each one religion, culture and belief. Once full and satisfied all our emotions, we will start to take a place in that great coliseum where "EVERYBODY WILL PRESENT AND LIVE THE LIFE OF EVERYONE LIKE EVERYONE WILL LIVE OUR LIFE". The author considers that this great objective is the main reason for the reason of our universe. For which it started with a great BIG BANG.

Mathematically and scientifically, it is accepted that in infinite past there were infinite Big Bang, as in our infinite future that will open infinite Big Bang.

Being "dark matter" the essence of existence, and being us part of that essence, our essence and existence that was not created from the "NOTHING", we will always exist in that immensity of the infinite eternity. For this existence of ours, there will never be "DEATH". Joyful eternal and cyclically we will be playing with our creation.

Details on some of the arguments presented

The origin of egocentrism

At some point in our youth, many of us had the egocentric fantasy that we are the only ones existing in the universe, and all that is tangible are simple "things" to indulge our "self". That after we die, everything around us will disappear, including the existence itself. Such reflect has been demonstrated by pharaohs, kings and now, many egocentric millionaires. I relate this theory with the intuition that, since we are all part of the One, individuals feel that, at some point, he is "the all", the "absolute self".

The sages of Greece always found the answer to everything. Using logical philosophy, they would evaluate the answers according to what seemed to be more genuine, and they dismissed what seemed to be unlikely. They would take as an example the assumption that the result of 2+3=5, and not 6 or 4. We cannot understand why we think in such way.

Greeks would attribute this to the "anamnesis" (Plato). They argue that this phenomenon is a way in which our self regains, by means of the memory, something we bring from our past existence. The egocentric person would remember the time he was a part of the One, and he is pleased to experience the instances when his "self" was still a part of it. He does not like feeling when he has to be one of the parts isolated from the One.

These philosophers also wondered how is it that we know mathematics; how can we have a concept of the all; the infinite; the nothing itself, our existence; how can our mind travel from one galaxy to the other in a flash; how can we be able to perceive the past, present and the future. All these capabilities belong to divine powers, not to simple humans created out of nothing. Therefore, Plato concludes that we are all part of the Creator. Absolute Pantheism. Thence they prove we all originate from an eternal existence.

The author presents these passages from our history to demonstrate that many of the ideas displayed here are not "crazy modern" ideas, but they have worried our forefathers as well, in profound thinking ways and it has lead them to meditate on them with a high sense of reasoning. I deduce that, to comprehend the concept of the beginning of the "all", there is millennial supporting evidence which confirms that everything existing must have been a "single entity".

The dark energy and dark matter of the universe are mathematically verifiable by astrophysics; hence, in our world of empirical realities, this is a reality. What is to some and what does it imply to others? According to the theory I have presented here, supported by an intuition that dates several millennia back in time, this energy would be something that always existed first, "a spirit or living soul, aware and conscientious of its eternal existence".

If we are considerably wise with approximately ten cubic centimeters of brain neurons, for how much should we multiply the reasoning capacity of our "Original Sphere" being its volume an entire cosmos? All its neurons are completely uniform. In this way, our One may separate a small fraction of its unity and allow autonomous behaviors and expertise. The first dark energy became dark matter through the heat generated by the galactic magnetic forces. Successively, the matter condensed into particles of the atom. The simple atoms started to condense forming the different elements of what we now know as the periodic table of elements. Finally, the molecules were structured with their complex formulas, enlisting to receive "the divine breath of life", suggested by Greek philosophers.

I consider that our Creator did not place in the brains of the biologists the possibility to decipher the secret of the transmission of "life" from the lifeless. This was done with the purpose of preventing the human to discover this data and depreciates in value and significance the creation.

The dark energy recalls the images and sounds of the past. If we observe some other galaxies apart from our own, some may be 5 billion light years away. Jupiter is one hour light away and the sun is only 9 minutes light away. This makes us think that a faraway galaxy may not exist anymore. It took 5 billion light years to have its image in our sight.

We are contemplating a past in our present. We see every day a sun from the past, 9 minutes older. The same occurs with the sound waves, but at a different speed. Could we state that this phenomenon verifies the fact that our "dark matter" has memory?

Should we obtain a shed that could travel in a few seconds at a 70 light years distance (the astrophysicists mathematicians affirm it could be possible to achieve if we manage to curve the flat factor in "time space"), from that distance, with a powerful telescope, we could see in real time World War II, and many of our old relatives, or maybe to ourselves, running as children in the backyards.

Another wonder conceded by our dark energy is that in "its environment", the reflection of images does not clash nor dissolve.

When we contemplate our Cosmos in a clear night, we can observe millions and millions of stellar lights; they all reach our sight at the same instant. Then, how is it possible that the images that come from North, South, East and from million different positions do not clash, deviate or dissolve in their paths? Nothing is "deleted", it all seems to remain as "memory". We share this behavior with the cell phone waves. In a stadium completely crowded with people using their devices, at a given time, there are thousands of waves communicating everywhere in our close and distant world.

Such wonder in which our "dark energy" allows them to travel through a means, with no interference, no blending, and above all saving them exactly as they are for almost an eternity must have an imaginary philosophical reason. In my opinion, this is to evidence everything that occurs, and later on, in our "Final Judgement" bring them as proof, to collaborate, present, confirm and reminiscence every biography.

~~

The purpose behind why we will all live the lives of us all, *vividly and equitably.*

This is an exceptional idea. But, how did it originate? I believe that the DNA of each race has powerful influence on every one of its descendants. I am a Chinese race descendant.

The construction of the "Great Wall of China" is a clear example that this race prefers to shut down so they can be left alone, and has no wishes to disturb anybody nor being disturbed.

For this reason, my race opted for a pacifist religion, one where the Creator is not constantly torturing or threatening them with infernos.

There have been other religions that have showed, for millennia, great satisfaction in conquering cities and decapitating all its inhabitants, from newborns to the old and disabled. Their DNA is so powerful that until this day they continue their beheading tradition.

By my pacifist DNA I concluded:

(1) that in the beginning of existence, it is logical that there only existed one singular being, as mindful of its existence as we feel our singular *soul*. Therefore, so as not to fall into the universal inertia, or "absolute tedium", He has to be continuously creating, through cycles (with beginnings and endings), not concluding in an "ultimate finale" (of eternal paradises or infernos).

(2) Its first action to perform this universal function would be to use the reproductive magic of the "ameba" (unicellular organism that when is divided into one or more parts, each piece regenerates as independent beings, maintaining all the features of its primary source. Therewith, I approve that we originate from our "eternal universal egg", and not from "the nothing", to which we will return sooner or later.

(3) When we all arrive to participate in the first theatrical performance, some may rise to be pharaohs, some others shall be slaves; some wealthy and fortunate, some others poor and miserable. How can the "original mother", then, welcome back all of her "children", without having to hear the claims for the injustice that one brother received better opportunities than the rest? However, should we all be given the opportunity to live the lives of all the rest, then we would accomplish an equitable justice. We disclose, with this, another mystery, understood by scientists as a real fact, but has apparently no 'raison d'être' or universal value.

They suggest that every matter of each being has an "antimatter". This antimatter is acting, in light of every action we perform, in another private "parallel universe". Our actions are, thence, copied as memories of each biography carried out. Scientists have met with these mysteries of the "antimatter" observing the physical reactions calculated by the actions which are presented in the investigations of galactic "black holes".

The author confides in the investigations of scientists, he considers them to be truthful and to serve as grounds to uphold his theory about where has each individual stored his memory in each private "antimatter universe", to later present it in his "Final Judgement".

At that moment, every member of the All will experience in real time, the "private universe" of each individual. In summary, what scientists assume supports my theory and gives veracity and credibility to it.

To suggest that the culmination of every event will be positive, just and peaceful, smooth as silk, has been an oriental custom for millennia, the reason for which this Chinese philosopher has selected from his imagination the exceptional and original closure of the universal chapter.

Why does suffering, joy and sorrow exist?

I remind you the passages devoted to Adan and Eve. I consider them to be remarks of that time, refined by wise philosophers and described in the way of parables. Its multiple interpretations portray considerably the most profound of human feelings. Tedium is countered by art and invigorating emotions. Among these we may name the unexplored adventures, interesting exchanges, affection with friends and family.

We should also name the artificial solutions, like alcohol, vices and, last but not least, drug consumption pattern. The latter removes, from the innermost of the human psyche, reactions that, at the same time, stem from the unusual activity of hormones and bodily senses, in order to suppress normal behavior and to boost what may produce fantasy dreams and hallucinations.

As an example, we have the successful "movie stars", celebrities, millionaires who have demonstrated to the public that, even when they "have it all", the complex of "Adan and Eve" reach them and make them turn to methods tilted by the artificial, in order to calm down. We, the public, enjoy watching Walt Disney movies in which a beautiful maiden is rescued from her life to be wed and taken in an enchanted carriage to a luxurious palace to live "happily ever after". As we grow, our preferences start to change from sweet and romantic love affairs to Shakespearian finales, tragic as Romeo and Juliet´s. Refining our preferences, we moved on to Alfred Hitchcock series, from the "London Ripper" we ended up with highly prohibited videos of tortures, abuses, beheadings in public... much more appreciated if it makes the client vomit.

But, since the public is curious and wants to know it all, this is mandatory reason to watch. The public is also interested in feeling it as close to their realities and fantasies as it can possibly be. By virtue of such art we encounter "best sellers" books and "Oscar movies, for their blockbuster success".

From another point of view, we have those who not only want to observe the activities displaying danger of death, but would rather participate in them as closely and excitingly as possible. Leading by example are bullfighters, bikers, Formula One drivers, Roman gladiators, "Russian roulette" gamblers, with guns loaded with a single bad luck bullet... As mentioned in the previous paragraph, the self represents, to some, reason for living when they feel foreign experiences; and to others, the reason would be stronger if they can feel in flesh and soul a near death experience, a peak of excitement.

Based on these facts, we may deduce that human nature compel us to create a biography. In every fact, we all participate in the cause of the events.

Therefore, if we all feel excited by a movie, because it allows us to "reincarnate in it", but, at the same time, when we leave the cinema we are still alive, in this fashion I believe it would be in our "Final Judgement" when we will enjoy, by means of each "intermediary", the pleasure of "existing" one more time.

This ceremony, where we all gather to pay the highest price to see what moves our emotions the most, be it the sweet Cinderella story or grim

London Ripper one, is proof of the desire we have of experiencing every possible life, maybe through stories or blockbuster movies or maybe even experiencing them vividly in our "Final Judgement".

For this reason, I ask all of you to elaborate a biography as interesting as possible, taking into account that what each of you build as an author, will be represented later by you as an actor.

Therefore, it would be convenient to include acts in our present lives which encase noble, charitable and comforting feelings. May them be positive to our fellows, since what we do to them, it will happen to ourselves as well, in our podium moment, at the end of the cycle.

Analysis of the author

This theory on existence is based upon the values of peace, equity, justice and conformity for all. It can be summarized with the following statements:

1. **The Origin of the All** stems from a single unique "point". Point of concentration of energy, according to scientists. Point named God, to some religious communities. Point or concentration of "everything existing", to many philosophers.

2. **The interpretation of that "starting point"** in connection with our existence revolves around IT (the Existence, the All), we are whether a part of it or we are different from it. The author believes in the first option. Contrariwise, I deem valid the mathematics of scientists, the reason for which I regard their theories about "antimatter" and "parallel universes identical to ours, but placed in a different dimension" as legitimate. I take this dividing advantage to assign one dimension to some and a different dimension to others.

Consequently, in both ideologies, we would have to share the current existence in this present dimension, so that, after we die, each can reincarnate in the dimension its faith convinced him to. This idea of the different dimensions does not oppose at all with my theory. I have mentioned it before as supporting evidence of my theory of justice for the peace of "the existence".

3. **Tolerance.** It is impossible to predict what others may do to us, but we may define what we would do for and to others. Intolerance is based upon justifying "imposing powers". Its 'raison d'être' has no convincing grounds of the truth. In the end, these "imposing powers" are executed to justify wars, massacres, abuses under "the reason" flag, having no reason at all. In my theory, I employ absolute tolerance to everything.

4. **Eternity.** To understand what "eternity" means and implies is one of the basis of my theory. For this, I rely once again in the "scientific truths" There have existed infinite *Big Bangs* prior to ours, and there will exist

hundreds more for all eternity. If this is verifiable by scientists, and understood by philosophers, then it is illogical that someone presents a theory about existence stamped with *"absolute finale"*, by the end of the book. Such egocentric book would only prove that the author is unable to accept the fact that someone else could write something at a later time. In such way, he would be the owner of "eternity", acknowledged by him and by all those who follow him and live in his supradimensional universe.

5. **Life.** I will not be able to use the help of scientists with this. There is only room for the philosophical thinking initiated by our descendants. They promote certain biblical events. In my theory, I regard such facts as faithful; however, due to their parables nature, we must find them different meanings. I have exhibited this with my interpretation of Adan and Eve and their original sin. I do admit that the Creator created "life" with them and descended to communicate. However, I interpret the original sin as an established consequence to solve the problem of

"tedium". Hand in hand with scientists, we have biologists. They discovered the DNA and helped us understand that this molecule transmits *life* from one being to his descendants. However, in my personal opinion, they will not be able to understand it well enough to be capable of reproducing it from an inert chemical matter, so as to produce "life" with a given DNA.

6. **Credibility.** I believe that, in the beginning, the Creator intervened more often in mankind, starting by Adan and Eve. Afterwards, I may believe his participation with Abraham, Moses, Jesus, Muhammad the prophet and more. None of them discredits my theory. They spoke through parables, though none left written proof. This matter has always been intentional, since every philosophy encompasses its true meaning and value in those who claim it, and more importantly, in those who receive it and wish to embrace it. Therefore, I do believe in the fact that this prophets communicate through their ordinances.

7. However, in order to place more value on their saying, they did not write any of it. In this way, they gave their parables greater value, for it to be more in line with the interpretation we each felt more consistent with their criteria. These prophecies are intended to make the noble ones seize their positive aspects, and the devious ones abuse their negative features.

We suffer, today, the terrible atrocities of these bullies. I urge the sufferers to release themselves of having to act and think as others compel them to. I thank the internet for giving the people a better access to the real truths. If you search "religious scams" you may see and hear recordings of these actual preachers of "evil".

If you hear someone say: "I am who represents you before God", do not be a victim; denounce them. Contribute to mankind attempt of being more intelligent (use the internet). We accomplish more and more every day. With IT we will be happier with ourselves and with those around us.

8. **Justice.** Many of us have wondered why some are born with a silver spoon in their mouth and some other are born under a bad sign. What we claim most to the Creator is why he professes to have created us "in his own image and likeliness". This bears resemblance to my theory, in which we all come from the same and equal source of existence. So, where does that leave diseases, suffering and death?

Some are more unfortunate and some are luckier. We try to present, here, the perfect solution to accomplish a perfect justice. I have contended that our entire creation is like a "game". All participants should create an original biography. Once we all return to the "Final Judgement", we will participate in all biographies as authors and then as leading actors in every play of all and for all. In this fashion, in the end of existence (closing performances), no participant may claim the Producer for having suffered more than others. Such perfect justice allows the creation of the following Big Bang or beginning of the succeeding cyclical event of our external existence.

9. **Morale.** The main foundations of "morale" is to ensure you make other people feel the way you wish to feel yourself. My theory does not only suggest we behave morally, but it presents a "mathematical reason" for which we "should" all do it, at our own convenience. We will do it because in the "Final Judgement" we will all experience every life vividly. Therefore, if we were to cause either good or evil upon our fellows, we would be causing it to ourselves as well. To conclude, this theory does not indicate something we ought to learn to be merciful; is what we should do for our own harvest of happiness.

***Which stages in our life help us reflect** upon a satisfactory solution?*

Our feelings never betray us. Many a time we are unable to explain ourselves why is it that we feel profound peace in listening to good music. Music elaborated in pacifist cultures and not with drums of savagery, obscenities and inspired in drugs and wars. While observing sunsets, shores with quiet seas, mountains free of human invasions, streets of overcrowded cities in a quiet holiday, without herds of people, these events speak to us and give us more answers than a thousand mentors, scientists, religious people or philosophers. These events slow down our heart rhythm and help us find more meaning in our souls.

We also feel inspired when we contemplate an infant, since they seem to activate energies of youth to enjoy life. In the same way, youngsters seek how to maximize the experiences with physical acts, natural or artificial. In the following stage we have adults who seek, by any means or jobs, to fix their economic future. Finally, we have those whose age make them consider retiring to a more peaceful life and, above all, try to feel pride in consciously fulfilling every act they accomplish every day.

About things in nature, I feel that, through our dark energy, we receive these messages in the same way every molecule of the landscapes complies with the transmission. These are the moments in which nature communicates with us to appreciate the art and artistic purposes of creation.

"In childhood" we witness, nostalgically, those times of sheer innocent smiles. We contemplate everything in awe, for it being "new things" never experienced before. Children run to touch everything before it is too late, since their parents will teach them that some of those things are not to play with, but to use in "serious matters, useful, finite, things that have reasons with no reasons".

I sense in this, that "our origin" place us in this earth to teach us, first, that the purpose of creation is to live happily playing. Later on, through the passage of time, while we walk absently, he ensures we encounter an infant to remind us of those lovely memories, almost lost in our minds.

In "youth" we reach our full physical potential, with the consequent boost of hormones and mental energy. Our energies over-excite our ego to the point of domination. More often than not it overwhelms us and some feel they need to recur to activate themselves with artificial stimulants. Their favorite music is "reggae", "hip hop", and any other that express vulgarities or savagery. In this way, we spend the best time our creation ever bestowed us with its "logical purpose of *youth, divine treasure*".

"In adulthood", when we feel tired of dancing, we come to sense the need to start saving for "old age". In this moment we strive to maximize our capabilities to struggle, mercilessly, to earn legitimately or illegitimately the most we can. As with youngsters, adults go astray with greed, ego-monopolistic actions, all so they can justify the expenses to hold their imaginary pharaonic life of many years ago. In my opinion, this last feeling is due to the light instinct of all human beings, even imaginary, that there is no logical reason for the arrival of death in our existence, therefore, the limitless enrichment is justified, as it is the idea that old age will never come.

"When we reach old age" we begin to appreciate melodies more attuned. We no longer run drifting like children, we no longer chase new emotions to experience like young people, where the disease of "tedium" forces to always seek the most stylish, in vogue, the most exciting.

Most elder people surrender to the idea that whatever time is left to live, it is not worth spending it seeking more wealth, but they should use it, instead, in looking for more personal satisfactions, especially things the money cannot buy. This impulse is common in "the age in which a person communicates the most with creation".

There are no words to describe what we encounter at this age, but we do realize, intuitively, that every time we come closer and closer from the truth.

About these last descriptions, I summarize: those of us who were lucky enough to explore everything with an infant innocence, those of us who have danced in pubs through the night and have had incredible adventures, those who have wished to fulfill the coffers of wealth and those who have defeated deathly diseases along the way, are entitled to say that we have earned the award of reaping the fruits of our efforts and fortunes.

While observing the sun go dusk in the horizon of our lives, is that we realize where all the answers are. We advert that when we see how when certain relatives and friends take their last breaths in life, we spot in their faces a hidden smile, for feeling that, in those moments, their intuition is illuminating the truth of all truths.

Those answers cannot be translated into words, but through their hidden smiles, they remind us that we once found them as well, in the moments of solitary and profound meditation, accomplished in a starry night, a fresh awakening, a day devoid of trouble, a sunset before a calmed sea, a green forest full of life and the presence of a noble background symphony, accompanying the beauty of our existence. This atmosphere places us face to face with the presence of the truth of all truths.

Even though there are no words to describe these events, our intuition gives us the peace we seek. Without awaiting any other opportunity, we jump to take a deep breath so as to keep such peace in the most profound corner of our soul. Once in possession of it, in time, we remove it from the deep of our breast, to hold it tight and take it with us in our last earthly breath. In this exact moment, our loved ones can contemplate our face expressing a joyful peace, revealing they have found "the answer" and that, in their companion, we move toward the mystery of our eternal existence.

~~~

Chapter II

THE AWAKENING OF MY LIFE

The awakening of my life

Panama and China:
my childhood experiences

To emphasize the theory mentioned before in which I state that the only essential purpose of our existence is to *tell* our biographies *vividly*, in our "final judgement", I shall anticipate one of the chapters in which I lived great moments, and which left as inerasable marks all my reactions, behaviors and philosophical beliefs of my present life.

I am the third of five brothers. I was born on May 10th, 1939 in a picturesque village, concealed in the tropical mountains of Panama. I was born with a silver spoon in my mouth and I never knew hunger or poverty. I grew up with good health and fortunate. When I turned six, World War II was ending. My parents decided to live in the recently liberated China. Exploiting the circumstances left by war, the money my family had would be multiplied a hundred times its purchase power. From being a slightly wealthy family in America, we became rich investors, with a textile factory with more than 500 workers.

In China, when I was 7 years old, during outings in the family estate, we would go up the mountains in caravans, sat in "kiaos" (wooden carts carried by servants). The maidens who walked at the front would light flares to repel wicked spirits and would sing beautiful traditional songs to accompany the sounds of birds and draw the good Gods of the intricate scenarios of the Far East.

This fantastic illusion of Marco Polo style adventures only lasted four years, until the last fall when we were covered by the dark cloud of communism. One side´s triumph is the rampant right of the soldiers in their victory. Their euphemism made them feel owners of the disturbances. In the first few days, I could observe all kinds of lootings and raids. The ancient sides were shot mercilessly in the street. Human history does not alter the outcomes neither during nor in the end of a war.

I participated in the triumphant school march and I was able to see in person the triumphant Mao and his escort, Deng Xiao Ping. I observed, after the first few days of the communist regime, how my family was treated and listed as a part of *the rich class*, being subjected to disrespects and humiliations from the plebs who vented themselves with insults, lootings and even murders of their previous employers.

Destiny helped us escape from China to Hong Kong, an English colony at that time (it became a part of China in 1999) as refugees, having only the garment we wore.

I was able to see in the innumerable control booths how soldiers looted whoever they wanted to and took whatever they were in the mood for. By governmental order, every book or text which was not communist was immediately confiscated and burnt.

Fortunately we arrived at Hong Kong, where we had to ask our family in America to lend us money for the flight back to Panama.

There, we started from scratch, economically speaking. Sooner rather than later, my father skills as an entrepreneur began to resurface the business and the family boat.

I received my education from the school La Salle, in the Panamanian capital, and I was deeply impressed by the religious sermons about charity, human values, heavenly rewards and condemnations to eternal and tortuous infernos. In religious justice I found the answer to all those atrocities and injustices that I had to endure when I was 10 years old, in the civil war of China. I struck a balance of all those events in which the evil people would go to the hottest infernos and the kind people, poor and unfortunate would be rewarded with the paradise of infinite joy. I was indoctrinated to the point of participating, as annual average, in more than 300 masses, all in which I received communion. In my spare time I would continue with my prayers, to which I blame now of being the main means of many a religions to stun and impoverish human capacity of reasoning, with the most cruel and unhealthy practice of *brainwashing*.

Berkeley: the awakening of my life

I started the University in California, Berkeley (UCB), United States, in 1960. In the first two years I suffered the effects of *brainwashing*. In those tortuous first years, I was so disrupted that I became a hypochondriac, and I got too many D´s and F´s in my academic grades. To make matters worse, I used to exchange letters with my friend Alfonso, who entered a theological seminar to become a Jesuit priest in Brazil. I, as an erratic beast in the hustle of civilization and logical thinking of such large university, wished to hide in a metaphorically inverse manner: from butterfly to worm, to enter and crawl into the Amazon Jungle.

Back in those days, I was lucky enough to listen to the teachings of a group later called "hippies". They would enjoy sunsets, when the sky and its landscapes displayed their best colors. It was a tradition that after a long hectic day of strict mental concentration, they would seize those moments to make small talk. Since the favorite topic back in the days was freedom of thought, one speaker told a story about his father.

He began describing that for several months his family had been visiting some relatives and, to board on the plane, they had to get up at 4:00 am. The boy said he was the first one to wake up so he went to call his father. The young man, affectionately, caressed his father´s back to wake him up and he rose like a spring, stand up and yelled: "God save Emperor Hirohito!" After the shock, caused by experiences suffered in World War II, his father found time to explain to his son about this psychological reaction, which had been long since it last appeared.

He told that when he was a Japanese prisoner, they would apply brainwashing technique to almost every captive. First of all, to have them become protectors of Japan and idolaters of Emperor Hirohito. Secondly, so they would not have free time to think or plan anything. Thirdly, to express their hatred toward the United States of America for being the main contributor to so many deaths, and to let them know that they would be the ones who, in their first carelessness, would go and kill them. With this, they obtained the main objectives of the brainwash: They were instilled to believe and repeat this dogmas; the more times the better. They had no spare time to think in any other logical matter.

They were threatened and intimidated with punishments if they were to do or think anything different from what was *suggested and taught*. The brainwash started by forcing them to repeat ten sentences in favor of Japan and insert one topic or something negative about the United States. Those who were heard speaking anything apart from those instructions, were whipped so cruelly that many of them died.

After repeating a thousand times, as it is common practice today with the religious rosaries, so many inconsistencies in one day, at night they would wake up one prisoner at random and he would immediately had to stand up and curse the United States or glorify the Emperor. The prisoner who would not wake up and express the *sentence* in three seconds, was whipped once for every second of delay.

So many and so frequent were their tasks of giving the *sentences*, that in the middle of the night, many of them dreamt and mumbled their *salvation duties*. In some cases, an unfortunate prisoner went mad and shouted from the top of his lungs, all day long and almost all night, the curses against the United States and the blessings to the Rising Sun.

Once the war was over, some of the prisoners had to be hospitalized in a mental hospital for having their minds completely disrupted due to the Japanese instructions. What can we expect from children who, from their mother´s womb, listen to religious chants and, then, have to mandatorily repeat such dogmas throughout every day of their existence? Under this condition we may ask ourselves if what was born was an actual human being with free will or it was a programed computer or robot built to comply with Machiavellian religious instructions.

This story of the *brainwash* had a crucial impact in my life. I used to walk completely blind through the path of reality.

I was a disrupted student. As a matter of fate, my student counselor recommended me to go and talk to a psychologist. With a single session, I was surprised with all the unreasonable events I was telling the doctor. At the end, this doctor told me that in this university environment I was completely out of my element. He recommended that the only solution for me was to drop out of college and take shelter in the hidden jungle of religion.

When I left the clinic, at 4:00 pm, I saw the sky dark and damp. I felt a profound inner scream: My *inner self* was crying desperately for me to change and save my life from that hole of despair.

I remember I closed my eyes in the middle of the street and placed my hands on top of a nearby car trunk. I shook my head violently to break free from all the religious mental wastes. Little by little, I started to raise my head and slowly open my eyes.

This time, I felt the metamorphosis in the right sense. I felt how, I departed from the worm and started to transform, feeling the evolution of my wings of freedom. I felt how, in my obstructed brain, there started to appear the sense of taste, so I could savor the nectar of true life. While I was opening my eyes, I could see the sky turning clearer and more excitingly brighter. The bustle of traffic became a symphony.

When I finished opening my eyes, I felt reborn in a real world, brimming with positivism. In the following days, I registered in my hypochondriac encyclopedia of the university hospital that instead of increasing the myopia every six months until having to use bottle base lenses, the eyeglass number started to decrease until I did not need them at all anymore, even until today. I was never ill again either.

My grades went from D´s to straight A´s and B´s. I finished graduation year being one of the only two students with perfect annual laboratory grades. I was able to go to dance, talk and feel in love.

My mind had the opportunity to participate in the first hippie movement, which started with the dogmas: *barefoot so that your foot´s soles can liberate and relish in the contact with nature.*

The first day, there were hundreds of followers, and the second day, I decided to be part, as well as the majority of the 30 thousand students, of the principle *to lose the ties, a symbol of restraint; to dress artistically and freely; to work only the necessary to live and not live for work; sex, as long as it is not commercial or without consent, it can be practiced in public, in broad daylight, because there is no animal, bird, insect or any other living creature who does not practice it naked.* It is not a sin!

This condition was later exposed in the book, *The Da Vinci Code*, in which it is presented to be a revered central act, for being one of the most significant *glories* of mankind.

This book comes to the conclusion that Jesus Christ had a normal life. Not being *normal* was a *sin* back in those days.

I was an extremely religious person. At the same time, I let myself be influenced by doctrinal ideas, but completely illogical ones. I was a complete social misfit, a failing student and psychologically hypochondriac.

By virtue of destiny and of the excellent intellectual environment in my University in Berkeley, California, from one moment to the next, I was able to alter completely my way of living.

I realized that religion had me brutalized, sick and with no hope of being a normal man. Only thinking in my own theory about existence helped me never to fear again for the two deaths (physical and spiritual). I began to obtain the highest grades in my studies. I won heavy lifting contests. I stop wearing, to this day, glasses.

With an open mind in a university like Berkeley, and studying Chemistry Science, never more, since the *day of my* awakening, I return to the religion I professed, much less to worship it.

Assisted by scientific logic, I started to shape my own theory about existence. Step by step I was able to use logic. Because of this sense of guilt, many a people stop living in order to give their life to a religious sect, for fear of the two deaths, which restrain and prevent them to accomplish many normal goals in real life.

Once I broke free of those fears, I was able to experience a massive and positive opening that has helped me achieve great success in business and in my social life. I was able to feel "madly in love" with a beautiful and slender young Guatemalan girl. Not all of us are lucky enough to experience this "madness" in our whole life; I was one of the lucky ones.

Nicaragua: the friends of the CIA

The second most profound experience in my life was a shipping event in Nicaragua. In 1969, my family owned a shrimp fishing fleet constituted by ten vessels in Guatemala and seven in Panama. My father and my older brother (who administered together the legal papers) were invited by General Anastasio Somoza, President at that time, to fish in Nicaraguan waters. We took the fleet, initially to fish shrimps for the President. His "perk" was the 10% of the raw product. It all worked perfectly well until the third month. He ceased paying for the shrimps for his exporting company. One afternoon, my brother and I were summoned to the presidential office. We were informed there, by Anastasio personally, who told us: "*Chinitos*, your boats are mine". I give you 24 hours to leave Nicaragua for good, don´t even think of doing anything strange.

After the threat, my partner and brother, César, took the first flight back. I walked backwards toward the door, with my head down between my shoulders. Deep down on my hunched chest, I could glimpse, with one of my feverish eyes, the unbelievable face with the same mask that most American presidents have, especially those pampered by the longstanding CIA of the United States, who disguise themselves in order to make fortunes, with no limitation nor aversion of their acts exercised with the power that the people, candid and suicidal, conferred to them. I crossed by car the border to El Salvador. Once there I recruited a group of guerrillas with whom I returned to Corinto port, in a small boat, through the mangroves. With surprise, we were able to disarm the guard at the entrance. We shot infinite times to keep all the rest locked down. They were shooting at as too, but the surprise factor helped us. We turned on the engines and made for Guatemala.

The following morning, two planes appeared out of nowhere and started to fire us. Thanks to the steel enamel material of the ships, we only took the marks of their shots as a souvenir of the adventure. Fortunately, we were able to fire back, and one bullet permeate into one of their turbines and made one of the planes fall. The second plane withdrew immediately.

The local newspaper published the entire episode at its convenience. The headline read: "CHINESE PIRATE CAMILO SIU ATTACKED CORINTO". I made a donation to my fellow companions of the guerrilla for the victory. I was congratulated by three emissaries of Cuba for my success in the Corinto episode and I was invited to participate in a movement to overthrow Anastasio Somoza, Nicaraguan dictator and protégée of the CIA.

My support was probably used to carry out a secret project. Soon after, the news broke in Paraguay that General Anastasio Somoza had been murdered with a bazooka projectile. Mankind achieved a just vengeance. Taking my mind out of absurd thoughts and trying to reorganize to figure out a logic project, I reached great economic and social success. I had an exporting fishery in Guatemala with more than 400 direct workers.

In Panama I installed a plastic bags factory with more than 150 workers. I managed to construct and install a steelmaking plant of blast furnaces for scrap metal smelting. I had 125 workers.

Today, I have a workshop with 50 technicians for the manufacturing of refine decorative structures, with our motto "to offer art plainly and details perfectly". In this craft I have come to be the best in the country, with pieces exposed in international movies, made for presidents, five star generals and the wealthiest families. I owe my success to the replacement of harmful thoughts, such as the ideas of one being guilty even before birth; of all natural things being evil and of having to wrap yourself with a veil of sacrifice and agony labeled with pessimism. I trade all that for the veil of positivism.

With the events in my biography, I have been able to demonstrate how several experiences, personal and philosophical, helped me achieved great success in life and in my contribution to mankind, as a businessman who provides source of employment, and for promoting and practicing art and creating a new concept of philosophy.

My home: the most wonderful experience in my life.

My life continued with great economic success. However, since what matters most to me is life as a human being with principles based on the experiences lived, I consider more important my private life than the life of the all itself. The world itself, as described in my following chapter, is on the way of disappearing in less than a century. The main cause is the world demographic growth, exponential and incontrollable. Followed by consumerism trends, the vanity of the most powerful, and those who believe they are "smarter" the more they boost their fortunes by means of corruption.

Today, after having a most fortunate life in my career, I can say that, for the closure of my biography, I can still sense my great prize.

My private life has had its best moments during my last 48 autumn years. My home has been blessed with the presence of my inseparable partner.

I have lived some of my best times at sea, and it has led me to regard my living with my wife as full of intense maritime emotions. We travelled almost around the whole world and we share those moments as if we had sailed through the seven seas. We have gone through many rising tides and some low tides as well.

We have undertaken some calmed waters with glowing sunrises; and some storms of bad moments that, through no fault but my own, I steered with whims and arrogance. I have also crossed the seas of "limited attention and importance to the YOU", for pure unreasonable pride. Finally, we sailed across the sea of hurricanes and witnessed other vessels succumb in the depth of divorce. We watched many friends and family drift away. I am grateful to my lovely partner for being on the steer, and for her bravery and extraordinary sacrifice, thanks to which we managed to cross successfully these troubled waters. I look back today, and I thank for being able to arrive to the port of peace, calm and wisdom. In the end I have been fortunate to dock my vessel of adventures and enter my cabin of retirement.

There, in the dining table, I find a warm dinner served with love and affection. Not far away, in the west window, near the horizon I contemplate the sun trying to rest from his long and tiresome journey of the day. Seizing the last beams of light that break through this home, I am fortunate enough to see the mother of my daughters dusting my fishing trophies, resignation trophies, humility trophies, trophies for saving the past, and trophies for learning "to care about what others care about". This is my way of thanking her for all the support she gave to accomplish this successful closure of our biographies.

And thus I expect to see, with the last beams of the day, the light of peace to inspire love in the soul of this accomplice who has walked by my side during the best time of my life.

~~~

Chapter III

We control us or we drown

Demography

We control ourselves
or we drown

In the second chapter I explained how certain traditional ideologies were misleading my life. I encourage all those who wish to change their way of living, to do so, just as I was able to, because anything is possible as long as we truly, reasonably, want to wake up from those misguided dreams. Personal whims or externally infused due to the lack of personal character. In the first chapter I presented my theory about the meaning of our absolute existence.

The third part of my book will deal with how deeply concerned I am about the well-being of the present and future human population, blind and leading to suicide. Since my theory believes that I *will live* the life of everyone, including of those who will live in this earth in the future, I feel a keen responsibility and a need to try and improve our own destiny.

The origin of the cause of all evil

The primary cause of evil is the influence of some religions and billionaires seeking their own personal interest. They gain greater economic benefits the larger the amount of people they can reach and obtain their goods and means. Religions deceive using whatever excuse, such as the need to bring many children because their God request them to.

There is no sacred book that reads be *fruitful and multiply* haphazardly. If the God of every religion is a symbol of perfection, it comes as no surprise that his sayings and wishes ought to be construed toward perfection of the human being. From the moment our planet hosted the very first life cells, no creature, plant or animal has ever multiplied frantically. Men have been the only species capable of dominating every other living creature, save for his own gender. Human gender is multiplying at a rate that in less than a hundred years there will be no free space to inhabit sanely, neither physically nor mentally. We have destroyed the climate and the environment relentlessly and rapidly, and many of us believe that we are on the verge of an imminent extinction, as we have caused in many other living creatures surrounding us.

I am deeply concerned about the demographic future, because I am certain that we will all have to share our good and bad destinies as individual beings.

When I was born (1939), the world population was of two billion inhabitants approximately. Today, we are seven billion and there is already shortage of land and water for food. The ratio of carbon dioxide increases by the minute in the air surrounding our planet, which alters the entire spherical climate.

The main forests, such as the Amazon and some others, are disappearing every minute by hectares commensurately with the increase of the population. Every day we see more rivers that no longer reach the sea, and many of the ones which do disgorge have already been strained by human use and have turned into black waters that cause even more harm to the fragile marine ecology.

I have a fifteen year-old granddaughter. What can this innocent child, or any other child of her age, expect for the forthcoming years, in about sixty years from now?

With more than twenty-eight billion people, inevitably, what would our frail Mother Earth be like? Is there any country or living movement of sensible people and leaders who is doing something to prevent this catastrophe? Not only will we have to endure scarcity of everything; psychologically, societies will degrade and apathy will rule among humans – natural disease due to the excess of occupants in a certain space, invading vital space of each human being. This phenomenon can be witnessed in people and animals that degrade themselves to the point of self-destruction, as a natural instinct.

Which is the purpose and what is the cause of demographic growth?

Every human being has the right and the responsibility to contribute to an existence with a good quality of life for the future of our generations. The question we should ask ourselves is whether demographic growth would help us today and in the future to be happier or if it would make us unhappier. The author assures that on the face of the current overpopulation, the ones who favor its expansion, will also be heightening the disgrace for all humankind. However, for each person who prevents this increase, the hope of sustainability of the human race toward beings living in harmony and in peace would improve.

Is it even a smart purpose for us to continue expanding? To what end? If there is even one. On the contrary, which would be the intended figure? I am shocked and equally concerned by the speeches of so many religious preachers who claim that this creation is a *valley of pain, suffering and tears.* If so, then why do they encourage the procreation of more human beings who were in the peace of inexistence or nothing? Those beings created, the majority of which will be doomed to an eternal inferno, will ask themselves in hell: who gave consent to the Creator to create us, with the result of condemning us to eternal suffering? And if that eternal punishment were to be the end, inflicted with no reason nor right, they would also ask themselves if their earthly parents, who procreate them, should also share the eternal punishment with them.

Therefore, if in the end suffering and error of existence shall fall upon us all, we could most certainly blame parents, grandparents, and we should ask ourselves if the original initiator of all this failure is also to be blamed.

I have said that those who exist now have the right to control our demographic growth, because the ones who have not been conceived should not have to be bred without the true desire of the ones who will create them (the parents). Certain religious communities think as if in some other galaxy there is people awaiting the turn to be created.

The truth is that these pending souls are not real. It is a human right and responsibility to be allowed to control the growth of the family. Every organization that intervenes to avoid *birth control* is the most harmful plague that is currently destroying our world.

It is exasperating to see groups, who once said the Sun revolved around the earth and that with their inquisitions proved to be the most terrifying and savage beasts that the human history has ever known, who burnt people alive, slowly, just to retain their properties, up to this day still be unable to admit that they are completely mistaken when they state that the demographic control only belongs to their gods and not to men, and if it were so, as I said before, no god has ever said *multiply frantically*.

It is necessary to know that, in all we can remember of human behavior, many needs have never found a solution. Every human disaster needs to be tended individually; merge them is only the excuse not to find a solution at all. The other group who has had a stingy reason to favor demographic growth are rulers, because the larger their people, the greater the arbitrary powers they will have. At the same level, we find the traders whose income goes hand in hand with the increase of consumers. I strongly believe that in the places where demographic growth is regulated, as it has been in China since 1979, all the afflictions started to find a balance. China has come today, 2016, to be the country with the best economy in the world, and that presents daily progress in social well-being.

Stop expanding so we can start living

I urge all of you on behalf of all the living beings that exist today, and of those already conceived, that we listen to our right to live. We, the beings that exist today, have more right to sustain with a better life than *all those* who have not been conceived. Therefore, in current circumstances, those not yet conceived with *no control* have no right to be born and alter the natural order. The unborn *with control* have the right to a legal birth.

It is a vital priority to conduct surveys at a regional and global level to measure public opinion on how people feel about the increase, curb or decrease of their region or world population.

Should the answer be *to curb*, then birth control practices, such as China's, ought to be implemented. The couple should have the right to have one child only. The second child will be *unwanted* and the parents should be punished with the loss of their jobs in government and become second-class citizens.

It was tradition, in China, to have families of seven to ten children; a very suited practice in light of the scarcity of human beings a hundred years ago.

With the *only child* tradition, we have witnessed a radical change with a new generation of children more loved by their parents, better cared and cherished, better educated and fed. The result is what it has been demonstrated to the world.

This generation of *only child* is superior to the old *brotherhood of ten.* Said society has proven to have the fastest economic growth, dominating the world economy at a ratio in which it is necessary to intentionally slow down so as not to unbalance future generations.

Deterring invasions

There exist, nowadays, societies which control their demographic growth. These societies must call out for their rights. One of their solutions and rights is that the land in which their great grandparents were born be left only to their descendants. I believe in the preservation of the organized groups. Especially, I believe in the truthful right of any group to gather, to live together (a home, a people, a country) and to defend their integrity by means of the prohibition of the entrance of illegal immigrants.

It is not a racist concept, antireligious nor against the democratic freedom. It is a concept of logical survival of a true democracy. I do not believe in the disorganized countries which do not control their population growth. This is indeed a toxic attitude and it should be punished by the other nations, forbidding the entrance of foreigners to their territories, just so they can invade and push their own nationals with demographic war (like a migratory bomb). Their famine and poverty consequences should only be observed from the distance by other countries so as not to make the same mistakes. Better have the self-destruction of one country for its mistaken practices than have other countries infected and cause destruction to mankind.

The restriction to immigration may seem cruel; but, wouldn´t you agree that the natives in a community, who have controlled their demographic growth and ecosystem, have more right to not being infected? What immigration right can the countries who have not ceased to procreate have? Do you honestly believe it is fair that some countries accept destructive contaminations of those who claim their right to procreate with no restriction, to crowd the streets with forsaken children and attribute all evil to society, to their neighboring countries or to their own government?

Abortion and sexual education

Why not dive into the root of all evil first? A real disease is the result of abortions. I shall explain this with an example.

In Central America alone, they perform more than two thousand abortions per day, and another two thousand are born *unplanned* or unwanted by their parents. This act damages deeply the morale and sense of life of those who *had to perform the abortion.* The *post abortion* effects are so psychologically severe that, in their minds, the fact of having agreed to murder a living child, completely alters the concept of respect and love for the lives of others and for themselves.

Instead of defending false human rights, we should urgently validate the rights of the organized human societies. We must have mandatory population control, foster it and educate about it at a global level. Every couple who only procreates one child should be rewarded.

This would benefit the reduction of population density. Couples who have a second child would be common citizens with no privileges and they should be soon sterilized. In the cases in which couples have a third child, they ought to be penalized and captured to have them sterilized permanently, so they no longer have the possibility to procreate ever again. Should they be foreigners, they will be expatriated for attempted invasion offence. Any further abnormality or diversion should be solved by the local law.

Our demographic control is completely chaotic. As proof that we have already exceeded ourselves in this limited piece of land, we may take the facts facing the detriment in world ecology.

The worst of them all are illegal immigrants. In the same way Spanish people, immunized against smallpox, would intentionally cause said disease to eradicate more than the 80% of indigenous population, what can we say of the African people who are already immunized against Ebola? It would take ten African carriers (as the conquerors did) to have more than 10 million people killed in New York in less than the first month.

What is more, we have contamination from cultures unsuitable for the receiving country.

In the Middle East, there are societies in which, for more than 5000 years, women did not have the right to learn to read or drive a car. Women can be raped and the guilty man is simply warned, a lesser punishment than the one applied for alcohol intoxication. In 2015, thousand foreigners were taken to Germany.

On December 31st, following their ancient tradition, thousands of them celebrated raping hundreds of German woman. Irrespective of the religion or culture of a foreigner, he should always abide by and respect the local culture. And here is where the unjust "human rights" defend the rapists for their right to follow their unethical cultures. The current deterioration is a cancer in progress toward total destruction.

There is no global organization which can deny the fact that by every hour and minute we are gradually degrading ourselves with the demographic growth, at a pace in which it is already possible to determine the few years we have left as humankind if we continue through this path. We are growing 250,000 peoples per day. Mankind degradation as a result of the degeneration of overpopulated societies can be verified with antisocial people, whose percentage is gradually augmenting. Every day we see more and more cases in which the very public guards, and particularly their immediate superiors, are involved in kidnappings, robberies, rapes and even murders.

Many ambassadors from countries used to be worshiped as very respectable persons who would come to help the host country. Today they are known as spy agents who seek profit for their country or their own interests. We witness today the disclosure of the frequent sexual abuse cases caused by many a clergy members, who used to be considered in high esteem, particularly those committed against children and teenagers. In the same vein, we have the *protectors of human rights* who, financed and bribed by unlawful and lawful mobs, misrepresent justice only in favor of wealthy criminals who will promise them an economic perk.

We see more and more cases in which the agent of justice is sentenced and the defendant indemnified with millions of dollars.

Who says that bringing more immigrants and establishing more industries is upgrading a country? If anything, isn´t it bringing more people contributing to the increase of needs, consumerism and worse social problems? Should a certain community need 100,000 man-hours for an agriculture harvest, don´t we always make the same mistake of taking *families* who in no time multiply and generate the need for schools, hospitals, food, housing and more, which, in sum, mean the creation of a negative figure of 200,000 man-hours of sheer needs?

If we were to ask the elder people in a town how they would compare past times with times today, many of them would say that they used to be a fishing village where everyone cared for and watched over each other. In beaches and seas, they owned everything and nothing would scarce. Everything changed with the arrival of *investors* who built large and luxurious hotels. Now, this very same fishermen see their seas with worn out products, and they have to walk through the beaches to *clean* garbage left by tourists. From being owners without shoes, televisions or appliances, they have become, today, uniformed slaves of investors. They used to have beaches and mountains as backyards, and their roof used to be the sky and the stars. Nowadays, they live in boxes, instead, with no backyard nor sky, those were exchanged by computers and electronic devices. They used to have their children and loved ones nearby and following their ancestors traditions.

Today, they do not know where their children are, because they taught them to be *miserable and unhappy*, and, in order to be *civilized*, they need to learn from their new friendships who know best about drugs, binges and abuses.

In the end, these poor, grey-haired old men are unable to understand how they fell into this modernization disgrace.

In summary, the fact that the greater the number of people in a certain space in earth, the quicker the deterioration and destruction of said region can be analyzed in any master in Sociology or

Anthropology. Furthermore, it is a bad addition to the entire system necessary for a future and stable life in the globe. Evidently, every day more and more countries approve the need of the use of contraceptive methods. Religious people have proven to be mistaken when it comes to physics sciences and social sciences. There is a large number of countries that have removed official support to religions for regarding them as the *opium of the people.* All the countries who have released themselves from this harmful burden have been able to enhance their social health and, thus, their economies.

A child should bring happiness, not misery

It is customary, that parents and relatives appreciate the joy of feeling *life renewed and filled with hopes* with the arrival and presence of a cherished child. To share and witness the life experience of an infant is to feel the reflection of mankind soul in the glory of pure innocence. Their smiles, mischiefs, ooze us with delight and tenderness that light on positive expectations in life. Above all, it affords us a sense of life that, with no arguments or eloquent philosophies, helps us understand the joy, bliss and the image of the purpose for which our existence was created.

I have been lucky enough to experience the reborn of many a feelings with the arrival of my granddaughter.

Through this tenderness, our subconscious relives the nuances of the true purposes of life. Children remind us that it is possible to indulge in delicious food and taste the exciting flavors. Their eyes embellish healthy minds with positivism, as if paradise was present.

All the other senses, such as hearing, the smoothness of touch, the temperature and the aromas, transport us to an illusions-made paradise. When we see a sweet child savoring a simple and insignificant candy with all his senses, we end up expressing our delight because we cannot hide feeling rejoice in experiencing once again, through this sweet child, what we have forgotten.

I sense we are born with honest feelings. In most cases we awake in the cozy arms of our mother who transmits us peace and security. When we open our eyes and gain other senses, we feel the welcoming in a paradise brimming with wonderful hues, exotic aromas, heavenly melodies and, especially, the dairy delight of our mother.

Smiling expressions cause us to find, in the rooted corners of our memory, the meaning of the word happiness. For this reason, it comes as no surprise that the grandparents would cancel every other personal commitment just to witness this rejuvenating event.

How nice is it to be able to share with them some ideas in which the level of attention and belief that the child pays to them is of a 100%.

Should we were to make a mistake with a child, there is no need to ask for forgiveness, we can remediate this in an instant with a simple smile, no need to hold grudges in the future. When they play with simple things, they manifest greater satisfaction than when an adult acquires a new vehicle or any other whim, only to prove his social superiority.

I mentioned this desire of feeling the renovations of our sentiments because it agrees with my theory in that the only purpose of our existence is simple and straightforward, just as the responsibilities of an infant.

There is no reason to try and give life a complex sense of slavery, because through the use of logic, we may earn a positively right existence for all infinity.

It is also impossible to believe why some religions try to have us assume that from the very instant we are born, we do it with a soiled heart, unworthy of existence and guilty of the original sin. It is not my intention to disparage the errors and guilt of any God.

My aim in this regard is to clarify logically this misguided concepts of the preachers when they speak on behalf of *God*. *They transmit* misconceptions or, even worse, they act through slyly premeditated intentions to alter concepts so as to benefit the so called *enlightened by God.*

Due to these contagious effects of such childhood happiness, the pleasure of having a large family was the right wish of a long time ago. This fact was valid 100 years ago. Today, we bitterly need to reduce our population in order to achieve the hope of enhancing the future, planned and wanted, to us and to our children. Otherwise, for each human being born more than a hundred primary trees will be destroyed, he will eat more than five tons of food and he will consume another five tons of non-renewable fossil fuel. He will add a ton of garbage to the municipal dump for every year of his life.

This innocent baby will continue to destroy a cubic hectare of air, water and sea. The reduction of these kinds of products have been for millennia the cause of war and disgrace.

What can we hope for future generations? Does no one want to shout to mankind, as I am, about this? Wouldn´t it be necessary to make a halt in the population growth of mankind? Isn´t demographic growth the main factor of the origin of poverty, violence and hatred among social classes?

We must attempt to improve the life of every existing human being. Many of us know that if we manage to cease growth, all the needs will start to remedy on their own. If we see a thousand orphan kids wandering on the streets, society will be able to find a solution for these kids before long.

However, what is truly sad is that, currently, when we provide help to the homes and community kitchens for these families, the following year we would find two thousand or more in this condition.

This way, every year there are a thousand children more, and with this growth ratio with no control, society or governments are not at fault for not being able to help, because it is absolutely impossible for them to win this race when the enemy (demographic explosion) is multiplying faster that solutions. Many theories are of no use in practice.

Results obtained by China with the "only child" legislation have proven to be several times more positive than expected.

The issue with religions and entrepreneurial lust

The main obstacle averting the world from salvation is the rules imposed by many religions and by the interests of plants and industries, in which every time the local and world population increases, so does their profit (real estate, car industry, schools, politics, means of communication, etc.).

Worst-case scenario, there are societies which are in battle plan and world conquest, which in order to impose their *order,* use in their social demonstrations a *calculated and planned militarism*. From inside their religious or ethnic communities, they are requested to procreate as many children as possible. It is the command for them to exceed the percentage in any country to be conquered.

Population growth is being used as a *weapon of mass destruction,* which by means of movements of people to other countries, increasing in number every time, start to remove nationals to the point of suffocating and turning them into minorities, in order to have them feel marginalized and cause their final disappearance. An undeniable example is the annihilation of many a pre-Columbian tribes (1492). Moreover, hasn´t history demonstrated the motives which caused the wars of the Catholic Church, Hitler or Milosevich, to *clean* an area of outsiders and guarantee life of the original race, so thus ensure a more stable future?

The root of all evil

I conclude this topic claiming that, whatever reason, purpose or neglect, the current rampant demographic explosion is the root of all evil. It is the path toward human self-destruction, as well as the eradication of the entire ecological order and of the balanced sustainable earthly system.

Should we be unable to reach a cure for this, then our Mother Earth will have no other choice but to punish us. She thinks as every atom in the universe do. Earth cannot endure our failures and let us destroy ourselves. She knows how to handle things more subtly. Our beloved mother will *spank us gently*, she shall send us mutated plagues such as avian influenza or Ebola, in order to have the necessary reduction of, at least, the 50% of the world population, who will have to leave this paradise through a fast track. As a final remedy, events foreseen in futuristic apocalyptic movies shall happen: atomic destruction. Inevitably, the proliferation of atomic destructive power increases every day.

Human species is imperiously degrading itself for its uncontrollable growth and incentive to action to suicidal fundamentalists.

With all of these flawed philosophies, which value more life after death, as in many religions, it would come as no surprise that one of the God *enlightened*, having atomic briefcases (which truly exist), commences his apocalyptic purposes. Nowadays, there is no single group of intelligent and sensible people who is aware that our demographic growth is psychologically finishing everything we have ever cultivated in this earth.

Erroneous official approaches

Unfortunately, due to careless groups of people, we are doomed to a terrible future to which they, for their ambitions and personal interests, have led us to.

Were the world to stop its demographic growth, no one could deny that more than 90% of poverty would disappear. Homeless children who suffer from abuse, would no longer be used to murder and to end up in the road to damnation. All their wrongs would be the first ones to disappear, with the help of their own societies.

The following has been strongly reckoned about human growth: the smartest and wealthiest people tend to have a single heir. Societies less financially intelligent, but slightly wealthy, tend to have two children.

Finally, there is the group who have no wish to use their mental capacity, the ones who have more than five children and those who have lost count on how many children they have tossed to inclemency.

This is the real reason for which I assert that, mathematically, population growth sullies society and augments disparity between rich and poor, intelligent and organized versus less-intelligent and disorganized.

We have pointed out we should not give the helpless food and shelter, but instead we should provide them with tools, such as fishing networks, hammers, shovels, hoes to sow, so they can become, in time, self-sustainable. In the same vein, I would state that instead of creating orphanages, community kitchens, it would be more humanitarian to teach, help and control them, as it was implemented in China, for them not to have an exaggerated amount of unwanted children. The demographic control achieved in China has been the greatest contribution that any country has ever furnished to world stability and human upgrading.

Law enforcement is necessary, because when humans gather in society is when they least reason for their own good. Furthermore, larger families are the ones who have less televisions, internet, radios and necessary means to hear about the real problems involving the fate of humankind.

Therefore, those in power, are responsible for regulating any abnormality that may harm their own environment.

Moreover, we ought to fight against religious people who psychologically punish with hell to those who use contraceptive methods and make no effort to have as many children as possible. They claim is their God´s will, who even came down to communicate it personally.

Military commanders, such as Hitler and Mussolini, in addition to the great international companies, rewarded those who had more children, because by doing so, they would have more soldiers in war and the big companies would have more slaves and consumers to gain greater profits. There is also interracial and ethnic wars, against which, writers such as Oriana Fallaci, from Italy, cried for the way in which in this modern time, they wage wars using movements of peoples which are being conquered. It is so unfair the fact that ten years ago, in Miami, United Sates, English was the official language, and now, natives cannot find a job because they do not know the almost statewide spoken language, Spanish! It is not fair the fact that many people from Europe, in which the day of rest was Sunday, now Saturday and Friday are also imposed because of the traditions of some foreign religions that are winning the war of *movements*!

The aims for power and war are incredibly resilient, in a social level as in an ethnic and economic level. There is no wish to stop this destructive and suicidal demographic growth.

Some other trends of the misguided global approaches are their means of looking for solutions to immediate problems. Many believe we should find solutions for economic, educational and other problems giving them false priority. Practically no organization wants to discuss the most important factors that determine the origin of all these evils.

They do not focus on the origin and main cause of the problem. For instance, if they have a thousand homeless children wandering in the streets, they are unable to see that the issue will not only be solved by helping improve their quality of life, but instead we should help avoid the procreation of more children because of their parents irresponsibility, for being ill-advised in their religions and unable to obtain from the government sexual education and physical help for their control. Multiplication has always been faster than the initial numbers to help.

Another misguided approach is to tell the people or a country that they need to increase their young population in order to sustain the elder one, due to their ancient retirement pension formulas and to the misconception that a person, by the time they reach a certain age, should no longer work. Economic growth, in order to make the wrongly balanced pension system feasible, should be achieved without increasing the population of any country.

Contrarily, if the distribution pyramid of the working classes continues the way it is, it would imply that humankind should have to maintain an exponential continuous growth, thus marching directly to absolute destruction. There are many elderly farmers to whom working in an estate, till the end of their days, would be not only pleasant but necessary.

Societies must find a solution for the need of their working distribution pyramid without having to increase the foundations of the structure. They should value and reinforce the superior part of said pyramid without ever making the mistake of needing a demographic growth.

The challenges of the forthcoming years

I conclude by making the following requests:

1. To search through the internet real data, verifiable and discussed in several means of communication. Our world is growing with more than a 100 million inhabitants per year. Statistics details, *only* for the year 2015, of the growth of some countries were: China: 6,801 million; India: 21,709 million; Nigeria: 5,262; Pakistan: 4,502; Syria: 0,585; Africa: 31,367; Arab countries: 10,156; Asia: 54,085, Europe: 2,093, Central America: 0,903.

From these samples, sociologists envisage that African society, already established in many countries, shall cover 51% of the world population for 2050, and more than 75% for 2100. Would it be just to let one society crowd all the rest societies out in certain countries?

I only consider just that a specific country (e.g. Japan) preserves, dominates and promotes its culture, religion and race locally.

They have every right and obligation not to permit entrance of illegal immigrants into the country, let alone with intentions of settling in it and displacing, with their descendants, the already existing population.

I do not approve invasions of illegal immigrants. Every country has its national anthem in which they sing to defend their freedom with their lives, as their grandparents did. Every country has its culture forged with the sacrifices of their forefathers. Almost every country in Europe fought and died for their cultural interests. France had to guillotine its kings. Russia had to execute the family of Czars. China had its civil war. The United States fought for their independence. Many are the countries which have had to execute their leaders for abuse of power. Nowadays, politicians, thousands of millionaires and religious people are abusing completely of the word *democracy*.

They use corruption, daily, in order to gain extreme inequalities. For all the abuse, I urge we raise our grandparents from their graves. Let us sing our anthems, not bail from our lands, and let us defend the land in which we were born. Let us be what our homeland prompt us to be bravely.

Let us fight for and with our lives. Alongside our grandparents, let us fight once again for a more just democracy.

We ought to remind *those abusing the power* that they are the ones who have besieged their countries. These peoples will deal with them the same way they dealt with the kings in France, the czars in Russia, corrupt democratic China and the rest of the countries which fought for their independencies, without running like cowards.

2. Another damaging situation for any country is to allow families of seven of more children. In Japan, whose population growth is a negative figure, the anti-socials percentage is close to zero.

The nursing for senior people has been solved without having to create more young people to sustain them. The world should emulate their costumes, because those are no longer theory, it is reality.

It is estimated that the population in China, due to its practice of the only child has ceased to increase 500 million in these last 30 years. Wasn´t it this reduction the greatest contribution to the decrease of CO2 in global climate? It has reduced a considerable amount of fossil fuel. It has prevented rural expansion with the corresponding needs of deforestation of primary forests, as it is happening in Brazil, where Amazon Forest has 45 less hectares on a daily basis. As a result, the model of China is not a theory, it is a reality that, in a few years, it has turned from being one of the five poorer countries in the world into being, today, the most vibrant, thriving, secure and rich economy in the planet.

3. In view of the continual absence of agreement among nations throughout history, it is necessary that every country protects its well-being by means of their own laws. Therefore, opinion on demography must be regional. Every country should decide by referendum their destiny, voted only by native citizens of that country. If the majority votes in favor of having control, then, laws similar to China´s ought to be applied. Minorities should not be listened to. In a truly democratic country, the will of the majority of national citizens is the one that must prevail, not the one of international religions, let alone the internationals which do not agree with the original culture.

4. We shall respect and legalize the rights of groups in societies or countries who wish to *heal* and uphold in *health* a specific space on this earth. Any social group, in light of the world´s lack of conscience of the serious uncontrolled issue of human demography, has full right to preserve the right of *group conservation.* I request to grant the right to any social group (home, city or country) to exclude any invader (foreigner) from their lands. It is a human right to defend a specific vital space of the planet earth, from which no stranger could be entitled to enter trespassing the borders to cause harm on it. This right would be the first significant step toward world salvation. Let us say no to illegal immigration, and then, yes to almost total reduction of immigrants, save for those who only arrive as tourists.

5. Intelligent countries (those who have ceased population growth) have to close their borders to those who do not control their demographic growth. It is against human morality that only because of the stubbornness and wicked wishes of invasion of some countries, others have to suffer their excesses.

I think that, the day in which a country were to be unable to eradicate its excesses collapses with overpopulation and suffers from epidemics, famines, and human degradation (reaching cannibalism), we, those who do believe in the logic of control, shall see them exterminate themselves because of their own stubborn thoughts. In the event of such situation, we ought to do nothing for them.

Mother Earth is wise and just. We shall not help them out only to contaminate our habitat. If some groups continue thinking the way they do today, it is responsibility of mankind to see that the results accentuate in some isolated countries and be stored in history as serious mistakes made by a specific misguided society.

Experiences shall attest to future humankind about the true limits we should all control in order to live in this earth for all the forthcoming centuries on behalf and as a right of humankind, especially for the rational ones who did apply the benevolent disciplines of non-human expansion.

6. I did not invent the law of Deng Xiao Ping (about the "only child"). Its implementation was pure prudence for the good of China and our planet. It has been the most important law and significant contribution to the world for the last two centuries. Every couple has the right to procreate a child. For the second child, they have no right, but they must suffer a minor punishment. For the third child, the couple must be captured to be sterilized. Women who wish to be sterilized, with or without children, shall see their voluntary contribution to mankind approved and subsided by government.

7. Scientifically and mathematically, human society is not dealing with certain problems correctly, such as: a) population ageing and its consequences; b) youngsters shortfall for labor workforce, and c) mayhem of social sustainability legislation due to the decrease of demographic proportion in the social pyramid.

No possible solution should suggest the need of demographic increase, because it would be a solution for the immediate present flicking through the immediate future. To say that demographic growth is indeed necessary is to confirm that our planet shall never be able to stop its demographic growth and that mathematically it is doomed to its own extinction.

Pensions legislation socially established need to be modified. It should raise from 65 to 70 years, and so on, increasing or decreasing depending on the health of each society and, particularly, its real economic sustainability.

My fellow elderly companions, let us not seek for solutions for our sustainability with more social benefits at an earlier age. This selfish thoughts will only gain us some few more years of luxuries, but in return, we will bring hell upon our descendants, an overpopulated environment crowded with unwelcomed strangers, a decadent future. From the afterlife, we will watch the paradise that we left behind turn into sewers filled with rats, where our descendants shall have to crawl as degrading animals in a continuous savage and immoral struggle for their subsistence.

8. Let us not foster the creation of more industries. Let us not spoil our people having them believe that the beaches at a "jet set" distance are better than the ones in our patios. Let us not encourage overseas tourism, because with the current ease of travelling and being anywhere in the world in a few hours, the conditions for deathly viruses mutations and short-term worldwide spreading increase, with the pandemic consequences that are being predicted.

Let us be conservationists and content. Let us refrain from telling indigenous communities and peasants that they are poor just because they have no shoes, washer machines, internet, bars and all the rest.

Let us not cause envy in our descendants, imposing them to dress in fashion, to consume more energy and, above all, to take vacations overseas because rumor has it that he who travels the most shall be happier.

The truth is that they will never be able to enjoy the real happiness and satisfactions that we have found in our own patios, as our grandparents did.

As a positivism sigh, in light of the so many errors which were being committed internationally, I feel grateful because the two countries where almost 80% of the best universities in the world are located, the towns with the most excellent college students have voted to start blocking illegal immigration.

Great Britain with the Brexit and the United States with its successful and smartest election of a president who opposes to illegal immigrants.

The same way we discuss about how societies with monarchies, democracies, communism, socialism have had their rights and wrongs, we discuss the World Bank, the FAO, human rights, religious Inquisitions and the other societies past and present.

They all have parts of their philosophies which are incredibly positive for the human well-being. The mistake in almost every one of them lies in the leader who interprets it. As an example we have the Bible and the Coran.

Both books are filled with positivism, but the way in which its interpreters classify a same passage has been cause of war until present days.

The word *bird*, may mean an eagle to some, a bird of paradise, a dove of peace, or a vulture of death. In conclusion, all of the abovementioned societies have made terrible mistakes. Inquisition was even worse than Hitler genocide.

Human rights are being disruptively interpreted by its representatives, as it occurs with the powers in the world banks, where laws of bribery and corruption are their concealed constitutions, only to make the rich richer and the poor poorer.

The author concludes that history has demonstrated that the *people has almost never been mistaken.* They made the right decisions in referendums as well as in presidential elections. In these views about world demography, I see with great expectations the movements against illegal immigrants.

I thank the decision of Great Britain for the Brexit, the presidential election of the United States in 2016, the movement against illegal immigrants that is rising up in France, I am grateful for all of them for their contribution to the global awakening regarding the responsibility of each country of safeguarding its demographic growth, starting by blocking all illegal immigrants whose countries think to have the right to invade with their population surplus to conquer and gain in this new "displacing invasion" war technique.

CAMILO AQUILES SIU CHAN

He was born on May 10, 1939 in Pesé, province of Herrera, Panamá. His family moved to China in 1946. Post war era and poverty of the majority of the population was more than a menace, because it was an opportunity to start new businesses. This is when his family installed a textile factory with 500 workers in China.

His elementary studies were done in Pui Chen School, Canton City, China. One of his greatest satisfactions was to participate in the student parade of the legendary Mao Tse Tung.

The expropriation of lands started, so under those circumstances his family decided to look for better life horizons and they escaped as refugees. Panama was the destiny that changed his life and the life of his family forever.

He followed his high school studies in La Salle school. After finishing he was accepted in the University of California, Berkeley, in the United States in 1960. He graduated as chemist, a discipline that had a protagonist role in his future.

His scientific knowledge represented a breakthrough in his way of observing and behaving in life.

Because of own will he abandoned the religion and became an enthusiast in the fields of science, astrophysics and especially philosophy.

He participated in the *hippy* peace and love movement which was typical of that time with all the expressions that had an impact in the worldwide youth.

When he came back to Panama he was in charge of the family business that his father started. Those were very difficult times in where only those that had discipline, organization and a peculiar sense of respect towards the tradition and culture triumphed. That is how the business started, with one fishing vessels that progressively ascended to 17 units with their own port, shipyard and processor used to export. With a clear future vision he created the first metal melt business of big ovens with more than 100 workers in Panama.

On the other hand, he was enthusiastic about a business in those uncertain times, so he established the plastic bag factory "Plásticos Generales S.A." that represents the biggest business coverage in its branch in Panama.

Another great commerce decision was *"Aceros Decorativos S.A."* known by the architects and businessmen as the one that offers the best designs and fineness.

The iron and other metals made possible to serve the requirements of his clients.

He is the father of two girls, grandfather, and a citizen that is worried and wants to help the scientific and philosophic investigation towards the most anguish diseases of modern times.

One of his favorite sports is fishing in the sea maybe because of the memories of those eastern seas that saw him leaving in a time that invited to deal with uncertainty.

He is a reader and tireless traveler and in every journey he learns life lessons from other cultures that he tries to apply to his family, business and philosophical environment.

Contact the author

For comments and observations:

E-mail: camilosiu@hotmail.com